FALLINGWATER

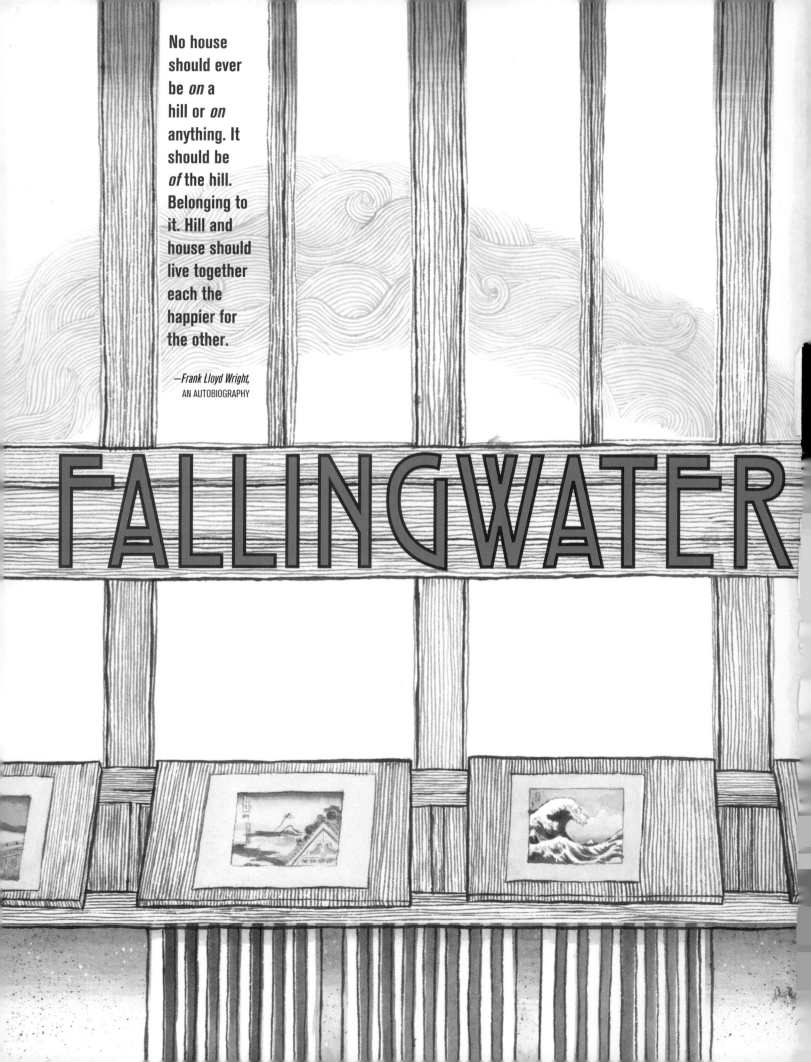

No house should ever be *on* a hill or *on* anything. It should be *of* the hill. Belonging to it. Hill and house should live together each the happier for the other.

—*Frank Lloyd Wright*, AN AUTOBIOGRAPHY

FALLINGWATER

Marc Harshman *and* Anna Egan Smucker

Art by LeUyen Pham

ROARING BROOK PRESS
NEW YORK

ONCE UPON A TIME ...

Frank Lloyd Wright was the most famous architect in the world.

But by 1934 he was just old. Someone even said he was dead!

He wasn't, but it had been years since he had built anything newsworthy.

A stream in Pennsylvania was about to change all that.

Flowing fast and cold,
tumbling over dark rocks,
between rugged hills
rushes a stream
called Bear Run.

In the office of his Pittsburgh department store,
Edgar Kaufmann thinks of building a new house.
Factory smoke whirls outside his window.
Streetcars' noisy clangs fill the air.
He writes a letter:

Dear Mr. Wright,
   I have a project in mind for you.
Please come for a visit.

"Welcome to Pittsburgh,"
Mr. Kaufmann says.
"But let's hurry. It's Bear Run
I *really* want you to see."

Wright hears the thunder of
a waterfall and sees rocks
stepping up a hillside;
sees water rushing over ledges
into pools below.

"Campfires have been built
on that big rock
for hundreds of years,"
Kaufmann says.

And Wright sees
that fire-lit rock
as the heart
of a house.

For a long time, Frank Lloyd Wright has dreamed
of building a house by a waterfall. Now he
will have his chance.

A week later, he writes to Kaufmann for maps showing every rock and tree, and says:

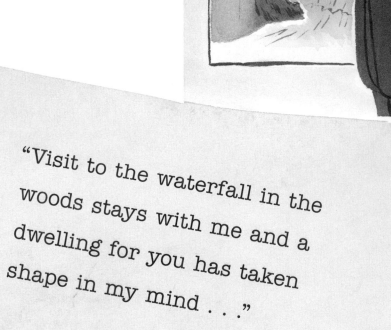

"Visit to the waterfall in the woods stays with me and a dwelling for you has taken shape in my mind . . ."

In the spring and summer
Wright comes to Bear Run
to look again and again
at the land and how the water falls.
The slopes are steep.
He will have to build *up*.
He imagines a tower.
From it and the rocky cliff
the house must grow.

Back in Wisconsin, Wright puts on his hat,
takes up his cane, and walks the countryside.
But he is not seeing Wisconsin.
He is seeing the falling waters of Bear Run.

In dreaming this house he will use everything
he has ever seen: stone walls from Wisconsin,
sand and adobe from the Southwest,
towers and trellises from Italy,
art prints from Japan.

HIGH RIDGE

And he wants to hear
the waterfall
in every room of the house
and to see sunlight fill every space.

CON

In his workroom, Wright studies the maps:
notes the stream, the falls, each rock and tree,
but he does not put pencil to paper—not yet.
Instead, he dreams . . .

It has been nine months since Wright
first saw Bear Run.

Mr. Kaufmann calls. He is in Wisconsin.
He is coming to visit.
He wants to see the plans.
He will arrive in two hours.
He is coming to see his new house!
Wright's assistants worry.
There are no plans,
and plans take months!

But Wright is ready. His dreams have made him ready.
He sees every boulder, tree, and waterfall.
He sees the house that will live among them.

His assistants are ready, too.
Big sheets of paper—ready.
Then . . .

Pencils flash!
Wright talks softly to himself.
Erase, erase!
Paper crumples, flies.
Pencils break.
Re-sharpen.
Lines cross, crisscross, connect.
Shapes appear—a house like no other—magic!

A house like no other,
where sun can shine,
where balconies fly,
where falling water
is heard from every room.

Wright finishes with a flourish.

Mr. Kaufmann knocks at the door.

"Our house
on
the waterfall."

"Yes!"

Kaufmann orders the quarry opened.
And within months
men with crowbars and mallets
begin to dig and haul sandstone
for this house like no other.

Pry and dig and lift,
stone upon stone upon stone.

Choose and fit and stack,
stone upon stone upon stone.

Workmen load rocks onto carts.
Others trim stones, chip them,
for walls growing higher,
walls like the hill's own stony ledges.

Sand, cement, gravel:
mix, mix,
pour.

Now concrete wings
and long, flat roofs
step up the hillside.

In the thundering water,
scaffolding spreads its spindly legs.

Like branches extending
from a tree,
the house stretches out over the falls.

Rock, concrete, glass,
stone tower three stories tall;

metal the red
of an old Indian pot.

The scaffolding is knocked away—

and the dream flies free,

soars over the water.

Never has there been such a house!

In December, the Kaufmanns move in.
At their holiday parties, pine branches
fill the house
with the smells of the forest.

Like a lantern glowing in the trees,
the house hangs in the darkness.

Wright visits in the spring.

In the early morning, before anyone is awake,
he explores the house he has named Fallingwater.

He sees
the living room
just as he dreamed it,
dark and low as a bear cave;

He listens,
and through the many windows comes
the music of water,
the tune always different,
always the same.

The trees, the stream, the waterfalls . . .
all still there.
And this house looking like it grew
right out of the rocks . . .
belonging.

the flagstone floor,
like wet rocks in a stream;
the large boulder jutting beside the fireplace,
the heart of the house,
just as he imagined on his very first visit.

Out on a terrace the moist air
swirls around him.
He leans over
as far as he
dares,
dreams . . .

And the house that flew, still flies,
over waters, under skies,
and somewhere, someone dreams
". . . so can I, so can I."

AUTHORS' NOTE

I think that it's the most beautiful place to ever go into and walk through that anyone could ever think of. Just imagine dreaming up a house like that! Because that's what it was like in the beginning. It was like a dream.
—Ruth Rugg McVay, daughter of a laborer at Fallingwater

Fallingwater is one of the most famous houses in the world. It was designed by the architect Frank Lloyd Wright for the Edgar J. Kaufmann family of Pittsburgh, Pennsylvania, where Kaufmann was the head of a large department store. He also had a cottage on Bear Run, a rhododendron-banked stream in the Laurel Highlands of southwestern Pennsylvania. Kaufmann's favorite place there was beside a waterfall. He and his family and friends picnicked on the rocks near it and swam in the pool at the base of the falls.

Wright was in his late sixties when he was contacted by Kaufmann to draw up plans for a new weekend house at Bear Run. It had been almost a dozen years since the completion of his last major project, the Imperial Hotel in Tokyo. He had once been recognized as the world's greatest architect, but such a long gap with no new buildings suggested that his career as an architect was over.

Kaufmann took Wright to visit Bear Run on December 18, 1934. Wright noted the large rock outcropping above the waterfall. The idea of building the house from this ledge and extending it over the falls seems to have come to him during that visit. Wright visited Bear Run several times the next year before he put his design for the house on paper. He believed an architect should fully imagine a structure before beginning to draw. He also believed that a building should "grow" from its site.

Having assumed that the house would be looking toward the waterfall, Kaufmann was surprised to learn of Wright's plan to place the house above the falls. But when Wright described his idea during a summer visit in 1935, Kaufmann excitedly agreed. On September 22 that same year, on a visit to Wright at Taliesin East, Wright's home and studio in Wisconsin, Kaufmann was finally presented with the floor plans for this house by the waterfall, this house that would be "a house like no other."

Kaufmann couldn't wait for construction to begin. He reopened the old Bear Run quarry even before the final plans arrived. This was during the Great Depression, when so many Americans were out of work. As many as eighteen masons were kept busy quarrying stone and hauling it to the building site. The more highly skilled men worked on the piles of stone stacked near the house, trimming them to size and layering them to form the house's unique, ledge-like walls.

Would the house hold or would it tumble into the creek as many engineers warned? Cracks did appear, but the house held. In 2002, to insure Fallingwater's stability, steel cables were inserted along the house's concrete beams.

At the age of seventy, Wright saw his career reborn by the acclaim he received for Fallingwater. He went on to design many other extraordinary buildings, including the Guggenheim Museum in New York City. He continued to work until 1959, when he died at the age of ninety-one.

Both Mr. and Mrs. Kaufmann died in the 1950s. In 1963, their son, Edgar Kaufmann, Jr., gave the house, its contents, and its grounds to the Western Pennsylvania Conservancy. Today, people come to Bear Run from all over the world to visit this famous house above the falling waters.

ARTIST'S NOTE

I have long been an admirer of the architecture of Frank Lloyd Wright, but my favorite among his buildings has always been Fallingwater. Of all those he designed, it is the one that best connects the structure to the environment. While visiting, I spent hours going over each of the rooms of the house, lingering on the terraces for as long as I was permitted, sketching on site as much as possible, and memorizing details of the exterior where cameras weren't allowed. I also spent days poring over architectural drawings, piecing together one level to another, struggling to understand the architectural language as best I could. Many thanks go to architect Patrick Gauvin for helping me through some of the stickier spots.

What I found most interesting about making this book, however, was having to reconstruct the building of this amazing house on paper. Few photos were taken during construction, and I would spend hours comparing the grainy images I could find to floor plans to decipher just what I was viewing. It made me appreciate all the more the difficulty of building a house such as this. The process of pouring the concrete into the terraces to construct the cantilevers alone is staggering, and I still feel the illustrations can't convey the difficulty of such a feat. I also discovered some of the unsung heroes essential to the construction of Fallingwater: Edgar Tafel, Bob Mosher, and contract builder Walter Hall, all of whom I've featured as often as I could in this book.

Frank Lloyd Wright was a controversial figure during his time and now. Reverence for his art, however, remains intact. It was his amazing sense of design, inspired greatly by his love of Japanese prints, that most influenced how I painted these images. His devotion to simple lines and clean treatment of materials—stone, glass, metal—has kept his buildings alive decades after their construction.

NOTES

Title page quotation is from Wright, *An Autobiography*, p. 168.

Quotation from Wright's letter to Kaufmann is paraphrased from correspondence in 1934. Frank Lloyd Wright Foundation Archives, Scottsdale, Arizona.

Quotation at the beginning of the Authors' Note is taken from a July 7, 1997, interview by Brian David Gregory, Fallingwater Oral History Project, Fallingwater Archives, Western Pennsylvania Conservancy.

BIBLIOGRAPHY

BOOKS

Hoffman, Donald. *Frank Lloyd Wright's Fallingwater: The House and Its History*. New York: Dover Publications, 1978.

Kaufmann, Edgar, Jr. *Fallingwater: A Frank Lloyd Wright Country House*. New York: Abbeville Press, 1986.

LaFontaine, Bruce. *Famous Buildings of Frank Lloyd Wright*. Mineola, N.Y.: Dover Publications, Inc., 1996. This is a coloring book that teachers/parents may be interested in.

Tafel, Edgar. *Years with Frank Lloyd Wright*. Mineola, N.Y.: Dover Publications, 1985. Reprint. Originally published as *Apprentice to Genius: Years with Frank Lloyd Wright*. New York: McGraw-Hill, 1979.

Toker, Franklin. *Fallingwater Rising: Frank Lloyd Wright, E. J. Kaufmann, and America's Most Extraordinary House*. New York: Knopf, 2005.

Waggoner, Lynda S., ed. *Fallingwater*. New York: Rizzoli. Reissue ed. 2016.

Waggoner, Lynda S. *Fallingwater: Frank Lloyd Wright's Romance with Nature*. New York: Fallingwater, Western Pennsylvania Conservancy in association with Universe. Reprint ed. 1996.

Wright, Frank Lloyd. *An Autobiography*. New York: Horizon Press, 1977.

WEBSITE

Fallingwater: Information about the house, the Kaufmann family, Frank Lloyd Wright, construction of the house, the land, tours, etc. can be found at fallingwater.org.

AUDIOVISUAL MATERIALS

The House on the Waterfall: The Story of Frank Lloyd Wright's Masterpiece. 27-minute documentary film. WQED Pittsburgh, 1987.

Vila, Cristobal. *Fallingwater*. Time-lapse 3D animation video reconstruction of the building of Fallingwater. Eterea Studios, 2007. Set to music from Bedřich Smetana's *The Moldau*. vimeo.com/802540

In memory of Andrew Schach, 1892–1967,
a mason for the Weltzheimer/Johnson House in Oberlin, Ohio, one of
Frank Lloyd Wright's Usonian houses, and grandfather to my wife, Cheryl
—M.H.

For Sally and Johnny
—A.E.S.

And with our gratitude to the Western Pennsylvania Conservancy
for their loving preservation and care of Fallingwater and their protection
and restoration of western Pennsylvania's natural resources
—M.H. and A.E.S.

To Patrick and Anouk, who make beautiful buildings
—L.P.

Text copyright © 2017 by Marc Harshman and Anna Egan Smucker
Illustrations copyright © 2017 by LeUyen Pham

Published by Roaring Brook Press
Roaring Brook Press is a division of Holtzbrinck Publishing Holdings Limited Partnership
175 Fifth Avenue, New York, NY 10010
mackids.com

This book is an independent work and is not endorsed by, sponsored by, or affiliated with
the Western Pennsylvania Conservancy, the current owner of Fallingwater
and associated intellectual property rights.

Library of Congress Cataloging-in-Publication Data
Names: Harshman, Marc, author. | Smucker, Anna Egan, author. | Pham, LeUyen,
  illustrator.
Title: Fallingwater / by Marc Harshman and Anna Egan Smucker ; illustrations
  by LeUyen Pham.
Description: First edition. | New York : Roaring Brook Press, 2017. |
  Audience: Ages 7–10.
Identifiers: LCCN 2016058236 | ISBN 9781596437180 (hardcover)
Subjects: LCSH: Fallingwater (Pa.)—Juvenile literature. | Wright, Frank
  Lloyd, 1867–1959—Juvenile literature. | Kauffman family—Homes and
  haunts—Pennsylvania—Juvenile literature.
Classification: LCC NA737.W7 H33 2017 | DDC 728/.372092—dc23
LC record available at https://lccn.loc.gov/2016058236

Our books may be purchased in bulk for promotional, educational, or business use. Please contact
your local bookseller or the Macmillan Corporate and Premium Sales Department at
(800) 221-7945 ext. 5442 or by e-mail at MacmillanSpecialMarkets@macmillan.com.

The illustrations in this book were created in watercolor, ink, and gouache, on Arches 300lb cold press paper.

First edition, 2017
Color separations by Bright Arts (H.K.) Ltd.
Printed in China by Toppan Leefung Printing Ltd.,
Dongguan City, Guangdong Province

1 3 5 7 9 10 8 6 4 2